TRANSFORM YOUR LIFE BECOME BEST VERSION OF YOURSELF

NIKKI SHEIKH

© *TRANSFORM YOUR LIFE BECOME BEST VERSION OF YOURSELF*
Nikki Sheikh
1st Edition

Publication Date: July 2023
Price: ₹299 | $ 15
ISBN: *978-93-5847-079-6*
Published by:
Adhyyan Books
Office No. 125,
Opposite Vivanta by Taj,
DDA SFS. Pocket-1, Dwarka,
Sec-22, New Delhi-110077
Website: http://adhyyanbooks.com
E-mail: contact@adhyyanbooks.com

Printed at: Repro Printers, Delhi

CONTENTS

CHAPTER 1
EVERYTHING IS ENERGY

When we look at the world around us, we see solid objects, but when we see it through a microscope, those objects are made up of tiny particles called atoms. And these atoms are constantly in motion, with electrons orbiting around a nucleus. This motion creates energy. So, everything, from the chair you're sitting on to the air you're breathing, is made up of these atoms; therefore, everything is energy. In fact, even our thoughts and emotions are forms of energy. It's a fascinating concept that shows us that we're all connected on a fundamental level.

Our thoughts and emotions have an energetic vibration that can influence the world around us. Scientific studies have shown that our beliefs and expectations can impact our physical response, and visualization can improve performance of a person in a tasks. This shows that the energy we put out into the world can attract similar energy back to us. Everything in the universe is connected, and there is a vast web of energy that links everything together. This is supported by the theory of quantum entanglement, which suggests that particles can become connected in such a way that their properties are linked, even when they are separated by vast distances.

Our thoughts and emotions have direct impact on the energy around us. When we focus our thoughts and emotions on what we want to manifest, we're essentially sending out a vibrational frequency ie signal that attracts similar energy back to us. This is often referred to as the law of attraction.

So, if you want to manifest your dreams, the first step is to get clear on what you want. Write down your goals and aspirations, and be very specific as possible. Then, focus on those desires with positive energy. Visualize yourself already having what you want, and feel the emotions associated with that manifestation - joy, excitement, gratitude. The more positive energy you put out, the more easily it will get manifested into your life.

Work on releasing any negative thoughts or limiting beliefs that might be blocking your manifestation. These negative thoughts and beliefs can create energetic resistance and make it more difficult to attract what you want. So, practice the techniques I have mentioned in this book and follow along. manifesting your dreams is all about aligning your thoughts and emotions with the energy of what you want. By doing so, you'll be able to manifest your desires into reality.

Thoughts are things

We are the creators of our own reality, and our thoughts are play a important role in this creation. Everything that we see around us, from the chair we sit on to the phone we use, was once just an idea in someone's mind. Our imagination is very powerful tool that can help us create anything we desire in our mind. However, it's important to remember that the physical manifestation of our desires may take some time to show up in our 3D world. It's important to stay consistent and not get discouraged if the results aren't showing up in our reality. We must choose our thoughts wisely, as they have the power to shape our reality. Every thought we think is creating our reality, so it's important to focus on positive and empowering thoughts to attract the reality we desire.

Napoleon Hill, a self-help author and motivational speaker, was a strong believer in the power of thoughts. In his book, "Think and Grow Rich," he wrote, "Whatever the mind can conceive and believe, it can achieve." Hill believed that our thoughts could either work for us or against us and that we have the power to control them. He argued that by having a clear and definite goal and consistently focusing our thoughts on that goal, we could manifest it into reality.

The concept of "thoughts are things" can also be observed in the field of quantum physics, where scientists have discovered that the observer has an impact on the observed reality. This implies that our thoughts and beliefs can influence the behaviour of subatomic particles and impact the physical world around us.

Neuroscientists have shown that our thoughts have a clear and quantifiable effect on our physical and mental health. Our thoughts can influence how we perceive the reality, how we interact with others, and how we react to life's challenges. By consciously choosing our thoughts, we can shape our reality and create the life we desire.

When we intentionally select our thoughts, we can use the power of our minds to manifest our hopes, dreams, and desires. We can harness the power of our thoughts to create our own reality and experience more joy, abundance, and peace. By practicing positive thinking, meditation, visualization, affirmations, and gratitude, we can take control of our lives and create our own reality.

The potency of thoughts has also been studied in the field of psychology. Cognitive-behavioral therapy (CBT) is a form of therapy that focuses on changing negative thoughts and beliefs to improve mental health. CBT operates based on the assumption that our thoughts, feelings, and behaviors are interconnected, and by changing our thoughts, we can change our emotions and actions.

LIKE ATTRACTS LIKE

We don't attract what we want, but rather, we attract what we are. This is because everything in the universe is made up of energy, vibrating at a particular frequency. This includes our thoughts, emotions, and beliefs. The energy we put out into the world is what we attract back to us.

If we want to attract something into our lives, we must align our energy with it. We must become a vibrational match to that thing or experience we desire. This is where the law of resonance comes into play. The law of resonance states that we attract the people, situations, and experiences that are in resonance with our own energy. fundamentally, we are the creators of our own reality, and by changing our energy, we can attract anything we desire.

If you want to harness the power of law of attraction, the first thing you need to do is examine your thoughts, emotions, and beliefs. And ask yourself Are they aligned with the things I desire? Or are they holding me back from attracting what I want? By shifting your energy to align with your desires, you can attract anything you desire into your life.

For example, if you want to attract abundance into your life, you must first align your energy with abundance. This means letting go of limiting beliefs about money and success that you might have been holding for years, and adopting a mindset of abundance and prosperity. By doing this, you become a vibrational match to abundance, and the law of resonance will bring you more abundance.

we are powerful creators of our own reality. By changing your energy, you can attract anything you desire into your life. So, let's align our energy with our desires and create the life we truly want to live.

CHAPTER 2

HOW BELIEF WORKS AND HOW YOU CAN CHANGE IT.

Beliefs have the power to shape our reality and influence our thoughts, emotions, and behavior. Our minds start to develop beliefs during early childhood and are influenced by our experiences, culture, upbringing, and education. In this article, we will explore how belief works and how you can change it to improve your life and achieve your goals.

Beliefs act as filters and interpreters of our experiences, much like lenses, shaping our perception of reality. They are not objective truths but subjective interpretations of reality based on our limited perspectives, biases, and assumptions. What we believe to be true influences what we see, hear, feel, and think, and determines how we respond to the world around us. As the saying goes, "We don't see things as they are, we see things as we are."

For example, Someone who believes it is difficult to make money may unknowingly prevent oneself from seeing and taking advantage of opportunities for financial success. They could adopt a mindset that prioritises difficulties and setbacks over prospective advantages. The idea that money is hard to get by might become self-fulfilling. This fosters a mindset of constraint and scarcity, which may make it harder for them to attract wealth and make a good living.

Changing your beliefs can result in positive changes in your life, but it takes awareness, introspection, and action. You may construct a new and empowering reality by altering your beliefs, which will also alter how you see yourself, how you see reality, and how you behave.

You must take the following actions in order to change your beliefs:

1. Identify the source of your beliefs: Start by becoming aware of your beliefs in different areas of your life, such as money, career, relationships, health, or spirituality. Write down your beliefs and notice how they affect your thoughts, emotions, and behavior.

Understand where your beliefs come from and how they were formed. Were they influenced by your family, peers, culture, or personal experiences? Recognize that beliefs can be changed and that you are not bound by your past.

2. Question your beliefs: become aware of your beliefs and question their validity. Ask yourself whether your beliefs are based on facts or assumptions and whether they are helping or hindering you. Challenge your beliefs with evidence and logic, and consider alternative perspectives.

CHALLENGE your beliefs by asking critical questions such as:

1) Is it true? do I definitely know that it's true?

2) How do I react when I think this thought? Who would I be without this thought?

3) When was the case when opposite of this was true? Find the situations when opposite of it was true.

By questioning your beliefs, you can uncover their validity, accuracy, and usefulness, and open up to new perspectives and possibilities You can use these questions to examine different facets of your life.

3. Replace limiting beliefs with empowering ones: Once you have identified your limiting beliefs, replace them with empowering ones that support your goals and values. For example, if you believe that you are not good enough, replace it with the belief that you are capable of learning and growing. Use positive affirmations and visualization to reinforce your new beliefs.

You can follow the below steps to replace a limiting belief

1. Identify a limiting belief or negative self-talk that's holding you back. For example, "I'm not good enough to succeed."

2. Choose a positive and empowering statement that counters the limiting belief. For example, "I am capable of achieving my goals and dreams."

3. Repeat the statement to yourself several times a day. You can say it out loud or silently in your mind.you can write it on paper and stick it near your mirror.

4. Visualize the statement as an anchor that's grounding you in a positive mindset.

5. Whenever you notice negative self-talk or limiting beliefs creeping in, use affirmations to shift your mindset.

Here are some examples of affirmations you can use to reprogram your mind with more powerful beliefs:

"I am capable of achieving my goals and dreams."
"I am deserving of love, happiness, and success."
"I am confident, courageous, and resilient."
"I trust myself and my abilities."
"I choose to focus on the positive and let go of negativity."

Affirmations can be about anything that reflects your aspirations and desires. For example, "I am capable," "I am confident," "I am successful," "I am worthy," "I am loved," "I am healthy," "I am happy," "I am at peace," or "I am grateful." Whatever affirmations your choose, it should be something that makes you feel good about yourself, inspires you to take action, and reminds you of your true potential.

CHAPTER 3
DELIBERATE CREATION (CO-CREATION)

We have the ability to sculpt our own reality since we are creators in this vast creation. As we play our individual parts, we should embrace the holy responsibility of co-creation. We should actively engage in how our lives and the world around us develop with purpose and intention. We may unlock our creative potential and bring about the manifestations of our desires through this intentional participation. Together, we can create a tapestry of life, carving out our own trajectories and adding to the process of creation as a whole.

Build Momentum

Taking action towards your goals is crucial for deliberate creation. It is not enough to simply think about what you want and hope it will come to you. You must take steps towards your desired outcome. This builds momentum and sends a message to the universe that you are serious about your intentions.

Often, negative emotions can be a call to action. If you feel frustrated or stuck, it may be a sign that you need to take a different approach. Instead of getting discouraged, use those negative emotions as fuel to take action. Remember that every step, no matter how small, counts towards your goal.

It can be helpful to create a plan of action and break it down into smaller, achievable steps. This way, you can track your progress and celebrate your successes along the way. Building momentum in this way can make the journey towards your goal feel more manageable and enjoyable.

Detach yourself from timeframe

It is important to detach yourself from the timeline. This means that you must trust the universe to bring you what you desire in its own time and in the way that is best for you.

Detachment can be challenging, especially when you have a strong desire for something. However, holding onto attachment and trying to control the outcome can actually block the manifestation process. When you let go and trust that the universe is working in your favor, you open yourself up to receiving what you truly desire.

you should not limit yourself to only one way of achieving your goal. There may be many paths that lead to your desired outcome, and it is important to be open to them. When you let go of attachment to a specific path, you allow yourself to be guided towards the easiest and most enjoyable way to reach your goal.

Have faith in oneself

You must have unwavering faith in yourself and in the universe. Doubt can be a significant barrier to achieving your goals. When you doubt yourself or your ability to create what you want, you send a mixed message to the universe. This can cause confusion and delay the manifestation process.

To cultivate certainty, it can be helpful to focus on your past successes. Remember times when you have achieved your goals and the positive outcomes that resulted. Use these memories to boost your confidence and remind yourself that you are capable of creating what you desire.

You can visualize yourself already having achieved your goal and feel the emotions associated with that. This creates a vibration that aligns with the frequency of your desire and helps to manifest it into your reality.

CHAPTER 4
POWER OF FOCUS AND THOUGHTS

POWER OF FOCUS

Our subconscious mind doesn't distinguish between positive and negative thoughts, nor does it have the ability to determine right from wrong. It simply acknowledges everything that exists. Therefore, it's impossible to stop thinking about something entirely; the only way to shift our focus is by intentionally redirecting our thoughts to something else. Additionally, our subconscious mind is unable to envision the absence of something. So, if we wish to avoid something, we should avoid dwelling on it and instead concentrate on what we desire.

You attract what you focus on, The things we think about and dwell upon have a significant impact on our lives.

If you want to avoid something in your reality, the simplest solution is to not think about it. However, most people tend to overcomplicate this concept. They continue to fixate on the things they dislike or don't want in their lives. This type of thinking is counterproductive because it only serves to bring more of those negative aspects into their reality.

This is where complaining comes in. When we complain, we are essentially focusing on the negative aspects of our lives and the things we don't have. As a result, we attract more negativity and lack into our lives.

On the other hand, having an attitude of gratitude can have a powerful impact on our lives. When we focus on the things we do have and express gratitude for them, we attract more positivity and abundance into our lives. This shift in focus can make a significant difference in our overall well-being and happiness.

The power of our thoughts cannot be understated. Our thoughts have the ability to shape our reality and impact our lives in significant ways. By being mindful of our thoughts and intentionally focusing on the positive aspects of our lives, we can attract more of what we desire into our reality. So, the next time you find yourself dwelling on the negative, try shifting your focus to the positive and see how it changes your perspective and your reality.

When you focus your energy and attention on a specific goal or desire, you are opening yourself up to the possibility of receiving it.

The first step in harnessing the power of law of attraction is to identify what it is that you truly want. This requires getting clear on your values and priorities, and understanding what brings you joy and fulfillment in life. Once you have a clear vision of what you want, you can begin to focus your energy and attention on achieving it.

Another important aspect of the power of focus is visualization. When you can see yourself achieving your goal or experiencing your desire, you are strengthening your energetic connection to it. Visualization techniques can involve creating a vision board, meditating on your desired outcome, or simply allowing yourself to daydream about the possibilities. By bringing your desires to life in your mind's eye, you are amplifying the power of your intention and attracting more of what you want into your life.

When you shift your focus towards gratitude and abundance, you are creating an energetic ripple effect that brings more positive experiences into your life. By acknowledging and celebrating the blessings in your life, you are sending a message to the universe that you are ready to receive even more.

POWER OF THOUGHT

Your thoughts hold the power to create your reality. It's important to recognize that the only thing you can control in life is your thoughts. By mastering your thoughts and learning to direct them intentionally, you can win the battle of creating the life you desire.

The energy, focus, creative visualization, and imagination you invest into your thoughts will eventually manifest into your reality. The more emotion you attach to your creative visualization, the greater the chances of it becoming your reality.

When you constantly think about something, you may unconsciously bring it into your reality. Therefore, it's essential to be mindful of your thoughts and focus your energy on positive outcomes. By doing so, you'll be able to channel your creative energy into manifesting your desired reality.

If you want to create the life you desire, the first step is to become aware of your thoughts. Pay attention to what you are thinking on a daily basis, and notice if your thoughts are mostly positive or negative. If you find that your thoughts are mostly negative, it's time to start changing them.

As we think, we create a vibrational frequency that sends out a signal to the universe, and the universe responds by bringing us experiences that match our thoughts.

Many people believe that they have no control over their lives and that everything that happens to them is simply a matter of luck or fate. However, this couldn't be further from the truth. We all have the power to create the life we want through the thoughts we think and the beliefs we hold.

One thing to keep in mind is that the universe responds to the energy behind your thoughts, not just the thoughts themselves. This means that it's not enough to simply think positive thoughts; you also need to feel positive emotions. When you think positive thoughts and feel positive emotions, you create a powerful energy that attracts positive experiences into your life.

On the other hand, if you focus on negative thoughts and feelings, you will attract negative experiences into your life. For example, if you are constantly worrying about money, you will attract more financial stress into your life. If you are always thinking about how much you hate your job, you will attract more dissatisfaction at work.

WHAT YOU RESIST PERSIST

The law of attraction states that we attract into our lives whatever we focus on, whether positive or negative. When we think and feel positively, we attract positive experiences and people into our lives. On the other hand, when we dwell on negative thoughts and emotions, we attract negative experiences and people.

The reason why what we resist persists is that resistance is still a form of focus. When we resist something, we are putting our energy and attention towards that thing, and the law of attraction doesn't differentiate between positive and negative focus. Therefore, the more we resist something, the more we are attracting it into our lives.

For example if you are struggling with financial difficulties, and you keep telling yourself that you don't want to be broke or that you hate being in debt, you are putting your energy and attention towards lack and scarcity. The more you resist your financial situation, the more it persists in your life.

So, how do we break the cycle of attracting what we don't want? The key is to shift our focus towards what we want, rather than what we don't want.

Below are a few examples of negative affirmations and how you can use positive ones's to replace it.

1. Negative affirmation: "I am not good enough."
Positive affirmation: "I am worthy and capable."

2. Negative affirmation: "I can't do this."
Positive affirmation: "I am capable of achieving my goals."

3. Negative affirmation: "I am always so stressed out."
Positive affirmation: "I am calm and relaxed."

4. Negative affirmation: "I never have enough time."
Positive affirmation: "I have all the time I need to accomplish my goals."

5. Negative affirmation: "I am so unhappy."
Positive affirmation: "I am grateful for all the blessings in my life."

6. Negative affirmation: "I am so bad at making decisions."
Positive affirmation: "I trust myself to make the best decisions for me."

7. Negative affirmation: "I will never find love."
Positive affirmation: "I am deserving of love and will attract the right person for me."

8. Negative affirmation: "I can't lose weight."
Positive affirmation: "I am committed to my health and making healthy choices."

FINDING CLARITY: KNOW YOUR WHY

When it comes to creating the life you desire, clarity is essential. But, simply knowing what you want in life is not enough. It's equally important to understand why you want it.

When you have clarity on what you want, your subconscious mind can work towards achieving it. However, without understanding the why behind it, your subconscious mind won't have the necessary direction and motivation to make it happen. The why provides the necessary context and meaning for your goals.

To give your subconscious mind the clarity it needs, take some time to reflect on your goals and ask yourself why you want to achieve them. Is it for financial stability, personal growth, or to improve your relationships? Whatever the reason may be, ensure that it's specific and meaningful to you.

When you have a clear understanding of the why, it becomes easier to focus your energy and efforts towards achieving your goals. The why provides the necessary motivation and helps you stay committed to your goals, even when the going gets tough.

It's important to note that finding clarity on what you want and why you want it is not a one-time event. As you grow and evolve, your goals and motivations may change. Therefore, it's essential to regularly review and update your goals to ensure they align with your current values and desires.

To start understanding your why, ask yourself some key questions.

- What motivates you?
- What do you enjoy doing?
- What are your passions?
- What are your values?
- What makes you feel fulfilled?

The answers to these questions can help you uncover your deeper purpose and understand why you want to do the things you do.

Take some time to write down what you want in every area of your life, including financial, relationships, health, and social. Once you have clarity on what you want and why you want it, the next step is to focus your energy and efforts towards making it a reality. Remember, clarity is power, and the more clarity you give to your subconscious mind, the better it can work towards achieving your goals.

CHAPTER 5
POWER OF WORDS

The power of words and affirmations go hand in hand. Whatever you speak is also affecting your reality. People often have the habit of saying negative things such as "I don't have enough money" or "I am very bad at this". All of these negative statements can also affect their reality because words have a frequency. Therefore, many of the things people say become their self-proclaimed destiny. It is important to be very careful with the words you use, and the emotions and intensity with which you express them.

THE POWER OF AFFIRMATIONS

Affirmations are a powerful tool for personal growth and self-improvement. They are positive statements that are repeated to ourselves in order to reinforce a positive mindset, build self-confidence, and attract success and abundance into our lives. In this article, we will explore the power of affirmations and how to use them effectively to achieve our goals.

Have you ever noticed the constant chatter in your mind, the internal dialogue that guides your actions and reactions? The thoughts and words you speak to yourself can have a powerful impact on your mental, emotional, and physical well-being. Unfortunately, it's easy to get caught up in negative self-talk, which can lead to self-doubt, anxiety, and stress. Even if you feel skeptical about affirmations, it's worth considering that you are already talking to yourself all the time, so why not use this inner voice to speak positive words and thoughts to yourself? Affirmations can be a simple yet effective tool to reprogram your mind towards a more positive and empowering outlook on life.

You can write affirmations for every area of your life. When creating affirmations, you have the option to be specific or more general. For example, if your goal is to earn a substantial amount of money, you could say, "I earn $10,000 per month," or choose to use a more general affirmation like, "I am happy and grateful that money comes to me easily and effortlessly." It's important to remember that what works for one person may not work for another, so it's important to find the approach that resonates with you and feels authentic to your personal beliefs and desires. You can then post it on a mirror or wall and say it aloud while looking in the mirror, or repeat it silently in your mind. Remember, repetition is essential. You can even record your affirmations and listen to them daily.

Initially, you may feel some resistance towards affirmations, and doubt whether they're effective or true. However, with time, this resistance will begin to dissipate.

Another way to use positive affirmations is by asking weighty questions. This technique involves asking questions that assume the desired outcome is already happening. For example, instead of saying "money comes to me easily and effortlessly," you could ask "why does money come to me so easily and effortlessly?" By asking the universe these questions, answers will come to you, and your subconscious mind will start to work towards manifesting the desired outcome.

"Don't speak negatively about yourself, even as a joke. Your body doesn't know the difference. Words are energy and they cast spells, that's why it's called spelling. Change the way you speak about yourself, and you can change your life."

— Bruce Lee

HOW TO USE AFFIRMATIONS

The key to using affirmations effectively is to make them specific, personal, and positive. Affirmations should be focused on our goals and desires and should reflect our own unique strengths and values.

Here are some tips for creating effective affirmations:

1. Be Specific: Affirmations should be specific and focused on our goals and desires. For example, if our goal is to improve our

health, we might use an affirmation like "I am strong, healthy, and full of energy."

2. Use Positive Language: Affirmations should be framed in positive language. Instead of saying "I am not afraid," we might say "I am brave and confident."

3. Make Them Personal: Affirmations should reflect our own unique strengths and values. For example, instead of using a generic affirmation like "I am successful," we might say "I am using my creativity and skills to build a successful career that is aligned with my values."

4. Repeat Them Often: Affirmations should be repeated often, ideally daily. This helps to reinforce positive beliefs and attitudes and creates a positive feedback loop in the brain.

Examples of Affirmations

Here are some examples of affirmations that can be used for different areas of life:

1. Health: "I am strong, healthy, and full of energy."

2. Relationships: "I am worthy of love and respect, and I attract loving and supportive relationships into my life."

3. Career: "I am using my talents and skills to build a successful and fulfilling career that aligns with my values."

4. Finances: "I am capable of managing my finances wisely and creating abundance in my life."

5. Personal Growth: "I am continually growing and evolving, and I embrace new opportunities for learning and self-improvement."

CHAPTER 6

SEEING IS ATTRACTION

Seeing is Attraction: The Power of Visualizing Your Desires

You attract what you see, what images you are feeding your mind are also creating your reality. If you are watching bad news on tv, not so good content on internet are changing your way of thinking and lowering your vibrations

Our thoughts and actions are heavily influenced by what we see, which is why it's important to select what you want to see in your day to day life. By surrounding yourself with positive influences, you can attract the things you want most in life.

Limiting your exposure to negative news and media can be an effective way to reduce stress and anxiety and promote a more positive outlook on life. Continuously browsing negative content can also lead to a negative cycle of thinking and emotions, which can be detrimental to your mental health and well-being.

Instead, make a conscious effort to seek out positive and uplifting content, such as motivational quotes, inspiring stories, and uplifting music. By feeding your minds with positive messages, you can attract more positive experiences and opportunities into your life.

Vision Board: The Art of Visualization

One of the best ways to attract you desired reality is by creating a vision board. A vision board is a collection of images, quotes, and affirmations that represent your goals and aspirations. It's a visual representation of the things you want to attract into your life. By looking at your vision board every day, you can manifest your desires into reality.

Creating a vision board is easy. All you need is a corkboard or a poster board, some magazines or printed images, and a glue stick. Start by thinking about your goals and desires. What do you want to achieve in your personal or professional life? What experiences do you want to have? Once you have a clear idea, start collecting images that represent these things. Arrange them on your board in a way that feels visually appealing to you. Then, hang your vision board in a place where you can see it every day.

By looking at this vision board regularly, you can program your subconscious mind to focus on those desires and work towards making them a reality.

The key to making a vision board work is to visualize yourself already having achieved your goals. By using your imagination to experience the feelings of success and abundance, you can activate the law of attraction and draw those experiences into your life. This can be done by taking time each day to look at your vision board and imagine that you have already achieved everything on it.you can look at your vision board first thing in the morning when you wake up and last thing at night when you sleep, this will program your subconscious mind to attract those things and experiences into your life much faster.

Role Models: The Power of Influence

Having a role model is essential if you aspire to achieve something significant and become a better version of yourself. A role model is someone who inspires you to be your best self. It's someone who embodies the qualities and characteristics that you admire and aspire to emulate. By having a role model, you can learn from their experiences and model their behavior in your own life.

The power of a role model lies in their influence on your thoughts and actions. When you surround yourself with positive influences, you're more likely to adopt positive habits and attitudes. You're also more likely to attract positive experiences into your life. A role model can help you see new possibilities and inspire you to pursue your dreams.

To find a role model, start by thinking about the qualities and characteristics that are important to you. Then, look for people who embody these qualities. They can be people you know personally, or people you admire from a distance. It's important to choose someone who inspires you and whose values align with yours.

Environment: The Power of Surroundings

Energy and Atmosphere: The energy and atmosphere within our home can greatly affect our thoughts and emotions. A clean, organized, and peaceful home can create a positive environment that supports clarity, focus, and a sense of well-being. On the other hand, a cluttered, chaotic, or negative home environment can contribute to scattered thinking, stress, and a lack of focus.

Belief Reinforcement: Our home environment can reinforce our beliefs and attitudes, which in turn impact the Law of Attraction. For example, if we surround ourselves with visual reminders, affirmations, or vision boards that reflect our desired outcomes, it can help reinforce positive beliefs and align our thoughts with our intentions. Conversely, an environment that is filled with negativity, limiting beliefs, or reminders of past failures may hinder our ability to manifest our desires.

Surrounding yourself with the right environment can help you get into the right mindset for success.

How people can influence our thinking and beliefs

the people we spend time with can also influence our thoughts and actions.let's dive deeper into it.

Energy and Vibrations: Every person emits their own energy and vibrations, which can either align or clash with our own. When we surround ourselves with positive, high-vibrational individuals who believe in our dreams and support our growth, their energy can uplift and inspire us. Their positive vibrations can contribute to raising our own vibrational frequency, making it easier to attract positive experiences. However, connecting with individuals who constantly radiate negativity, doubt, or fear can lower our vibration and make it challenging to manifest our desires.

Belief Systems and Limiting Beliefs: The people we spend time with often shape our belief systems and can either reinforce or challenge our limiting beliefs. If we surround ourselves with individuals who believe in abundance, success, and possibilities, their beliefs can help us expand our own mindset and strengthen our ability to attract what we desire. Conversely, being around people who hold limiting beliefs, constantly doubt our abilities, or discourage our dreams can undermine our confidence and hinder our manifestation process.

Emotional State and Support: The emotional state of those around us can influence our own emotional well-being and, consequently, impact our ability to manifest. When we connect with people who are supportive, encouraging, and positive, their emotional support can uplift us during challenging times and reinforce our belief in our desires. However, engaging with individuals who drain our energy, create drama, or consistently bring negativity into our lives can hinder our progress and make it difficult to maintain a positive mindset necessary for successful manifestation.

Alignment with Goals and Values: The people we surround ourselves with should ideally align with our goals, values, and aspirations. When we connect with like-minded individuals who share similar visions and desires, we can create a supportive network that inspires and motivates us. Being around individuals who align with our values can create a harmonious environment where growth and manifestation are nurtured. Conversely, relationships with people who constantly undermine our goals, have conflicting values, or hold us back can create resistance and hinder our ability to attract what we truly desire.

While it may be challenging, sometimes it is necessary to remove certain people from our lives to support our manifestation process. If someone consistently brings negativity, doubt, or toxic energy into our lives, it can hinder our progress and impede our ability to align with the Law of Attraction. By distancing ourselves from such individuals, we create space for more positive and supportive connections to enter our lives, enhancing our ability to attract and manifest our desires.

CHAPTER 7
POWER OF CONSISTENCY AND CLARITY IN MIND

CLARITY IN MIND

One of the fundamental aspects of crafting the life you desire is gaining clarity about your goals and aspirations. It is essential to have a clear understanding of what you want and why you want it. By defining your desires with precision, you set a solid foundation for your journey towards fulfillment. There are various ways to achieve clarity in life. Spending quality time alone allows you to reflect, introspect, and gain insights into your true desires. Nature has a remarkable ability to calm the mind and provide clarity. Immersing yourself in natural surroundings can help you gain perspective and connect with your inner self. Additionally, practicing meditation can quiet the noise of daily life, allowing your mind to settle and bringing clarity to your thoughts and intentions. Embracing these practices will help you cultivate the clarity needed to navigate your path towards a fulfilling life.

Once you have determined what you want in life, it becomes crucial to create a blueprint that outlines how you can achieve your desired outcomes. This blueprint serves as a roadmap, guiding you towards your goals and providing a clear path to follow. By mapping out the necessary steps, actions, and strategies, you can move forward with purpose and intention.

In the pursuit of your goals, commitment becomes an alternative to blind faith. It is through your unwavering commitment that you stay dedicated and focused on your blueprint. Rather than solely relying on faith, which can be uncertain, commitment ensures that you take consistent action towards your desired outcomes. It keeps you motivated, persevering even when faced with obstacles or setbacks along the way.

To effectively create your blueprint, it is essential to maintain a steady stream of thought. This involves continuously refining and revisiting your plan, adapting it as needed, and staying open to new possibilities. Regularly assessing your progress, adjusting strategies, and staying flexible allows you to make informed decisions and stay on track towards your goals.

CONSISTENCY

If you want to see results in your life, consistency is the secret sauce! Without it, achieving your goals becomes quite a challenge. Just think about it: if you want to build a muscular body, you need to hit the gym regularly and stick to your workout routine. And if shedding those extra pounds is your aim, being mindful of what and how much you eat consistently is key to maintaining a healthy lifestyle.

The same principle applies to topping exams. You've got to study consistently, dedicating regular time and effort to grasp the material and prepare effectively. It's not just about last-minute cramming but about consistent learning and revision that truly helps you excel.

And if you're on the job hunt, being consistent in applying for positions and showing up for interviews will eventually land you that dream job you've been eyeing. It's about staying motivated and persistent, even when faced with rejections or setbacks.

Remember, consistency is the key that unlocks the door to success in everything you do. So, if you truly want to achieve something remarkable, be unwavering in your efforts and stay consistent. Take inspiration from the legendary Thomas Edison, who failed a thousand times while inventing the light bulb. When asked about those failures, he famously said, "I didn't fail a thousand times. The light bulb was an invention with a thousand steps." His perseverance and consistency ultimately led to one of the greatest inventions in history.

CHAPTER 8
POWER OF GRATITUDE

Gratitude is a powerful tool that can help you manifest more abundance in your life. The reason why gratitude is so powerful is because everything in the universe operates on a vibration, and gratitude is a vibration. When you express gratitude, you emit the vibration of having something you feel complete, even if you don't have it yet. This vibration attracts more abundance into your life and can help you manifest what you want.

To harness the power of gratitude, you must start by pausing and looking around you. Take a moment to appreciate everything you have in your life, from your phone and your computer to your bed and toothbrush. It's essential to cultivate a daily gratitude practice by taking two to three minutes every morning to think about the good things in your life and be thankful for them.

At first, it might be challenging to focus on the positive things in your life, especially if your brain's neural pathways are wired to focus on the negative. However, with practice, you can rewire your brain and start to wake up feeling grateful every day without even trying.

The more you practice gratitude, the more you will put yourself into the reality of having more. When you're in an abundant state, you attract more abundance into your life. For example, if you're grateful for the money you have now, you'll attract more money into your life.

It's important to remember that everything in your world operates by law, including the law of rhythm. There may be moments when life's rhythm takes a downward turn and it appears that everything is going against you, but if you keep your attitude right, everything will turn out right in the end.

Practice gratitude daily by starting your day with a few minutes of reflection. Lay in bed and think about all the good things in your life, big or small, that you're grateful for. Train your brain to look for the positive instead of the negative.

Maintaining a state of appreciation or having an attitude of gratitude is incredibly powerful and can elevate your vibrational frequency to its highest level. By shifting your focus from what you lack to what you already have, you can alter your perception of reality.

To develop this habit, try starting each morning by writing in a gratitude journal. One of the best ways to cultivate gratitude is through journaling.

Journaling is the practice of writing down our thoughts and emotions in a private journal. It is a powerful tool for self-reflection, self-expression, and personal growth. Journaling helps us to connect with our inner selves, gain insights into our thought processes, and become more mindful of our emotions.

Take a pen and paper and jot down all the things you are thankful for in your life. Then, write down everything you wish to manifest in your life. The more gratitude you have, the more abundance you will attract into your life.

Make a list of at least 10 things in your life right now that you're grateful for. Take your time and be specific. Focus on what you have, not what you lack. This will help you feel abundant and attract more abundance into your life.

Send love to three people who are hurting or causing you problems. Don't do it for their benefit, do it for yours. The energy you put out into the universe will come back to you.

FOCUS ON THE PRESENT MOMENT

- When you are reflecting on the things that you are grateful for, try to focus on the present moment. Pay attention to the sights, sounds, and sensations around you. This can help to cultivate a sense of mindfulness and presence, which can enhance the power of your gratitude practice.

- Pause and take a moment to look around you, wherever you are. Notice the things you can see, hear, or touch. Everything in our reality is a vibration, and gratitude is a vibration too. When you give off gratitude, you emit the vibration of having something you feel complete, even if it's not physically present.

• Spend five minutes in quiet meditation and ask for direction from the universe or spirit. Trust that the answers will come to you in their own time. This simple practice can work wonders whenever you're having problems.

BE SPECIFIC

When you are writing in your gratitude journal, be as specific as possible. Instead of simply writing "I am grateful for my family," try to identify specific qualities or actions that you appreciate about each family member. This will help to deepen your sense of gratitude and appreciation.

MAKE IT A DAILY HABIT

One of the keys to success with gratitude journaling is to make it a daily habit. Set aside a few minutes each day to reflect on the things that you are grateful for and write them down in your journal. Consistency is key when it comes to developing any new habit, and gratitude journaling is no exception.

You can use gratitude journal to enhance various aspects of your life.

TO REDUCES STRESS

Gratitude journaling can help to reduce stress levels by shifting our focus from negative thoughts to positive ones. It helps us to recognize the good things in our lives and appreciate them, even in the midst of challenging situations. When we practice gratitude journaling, we are training our minds to focus on the positive, which can help to reduce stress and anxiety.

INCREASE HAPPINESS

Gratitude journaling can also increase our overall happiness and well-being. By focusing on the good things in our lives, we are reminding ourselves of the positive aspects of our existence. This can help us to feel more content and satisfied with our lives, even during difficult times.

IMPROVE RELATIONSHIPS

Gratitude journaling can also help to improve our relationships with others. When we focus on the good things in our lives, we are more likely to see the positive qualities in others as well. This can help us to build stronger, more positive relationships with the people around us.

ENHANCE SELF-AWARENESS

Gratitude journaling can also help us to become more self-aware. When we take the time to reflect on the things that we are grateful for, we are gaining insights into our own values, beliefs, and priorities. This can help us to become more aware of our own emotions and motivations, which can lead to greater self-understanding and personal growth.

CHAPTER 9
IDENTITY SHIFT A POWERFUL PRACTICE (SELF IMAGE)

Identity Shift: A Powerful Practice for Improving Self-Image

How you perceive yourself can greatly influence the type of people you attract, the experiences you have, and the opportunities that come your way.If you are not happy with the outcomes you are experiencing in life, then it may be time to focus on an identity shift.

So first off, what is identity? Identity is the way that we perceive ourselves. It's the way that we see ourselves in the world, and it's also the way that we see the world around us. It's very important to recognize that our identity is something that we can change. It's not set in stone, and we can shift it at any time.

Your identity is essentially the core of who you are as a person. It's how you perceive yourself, including your thoughts, feelings, and actions. Your values are also a key part of your identity, as they guide your decisions and actions in life. Your beliefs and the stories you tell yourself about your past experiences also play a significant role in shaping your identity. By understanding these aspects of your identity, you can gain a better understanding of yourself and make more informed decisions about how to live your life.

Values are the principles and beliefs that you hold dear and that guide your actions and decisions. Your identity represents your sense of self, which includes how you think, act, and feel about yourself, as well as your personal values. Your identity is like your comfort zone, and many people are hesitant to change their identity because they fear stepping out of their comfort zone. However, shifting your identity is not about leaving your comfort zone but rather expanding it. As you shift your identity, you create a new reality and transform the energy that you put out into the world. By becoming aware of your inner self-image, you can take steps to shift your identity and live a more fulfilling life. Over time, your new identity becomes your new comfort zone, and you can continue to grow and evolve as a person.

This shift can have a profound impact on your life, creating a completely new reflection of yourself. As you shift your identity, you also shift the energy you put out into the world. This can create a ripple effect that transforms your entire reality, bringing in new people, experiences, and opportunities that align with your new identity. This transformation occurs from the inside out, and you may find yourself feeling more confident, motivated, and inspired as you move forward with your new identity. By embracing this shift, you can create a new and exciting chapter in your life.

You Attract Who You Are

If you take a moment to think about the people who are most present in your life, you may notice that you have many things in common with them. This is because, at a fundamental level, we tend to attract people who share our values, beliefs, and energy. If you are struggling to find supportive, positive people in your life, then it may be time to examine your self-image and make some changes.

To attract positive, like-minded people into your life, you need to become the kind of person that you want to attract. This means that you need to cultivate positive qualities and characteristics within yourself, such as confidence, kindness, and generosity. When you embody these traits, you will naturally attract people who value and appreciate these qualities.

Furthermore, if you are looking to make a career change or start a business, it is important to focus on becoming the kind of person that your ideal client or employer would want to work with. By improving your self-image and developing your skills and expertise, you will naturally attract opportunities that align with your values and goals.

How we shift our identity

1. Become aware of your self-image: This involves reflecting on how you see yourself, how you carry yourself, your body language, and the story you tell yourself about who you are. Ask yourself questions such as,

"What is my self-image?",
"How do I see myself?",
"How do I carry myself?", and
"What is the story I keep telling myself about who I am?"

2. Identify the version of yourself you want to be: Think about the qualities and traits of the person you want to become. For example, you may want to become a top-selling salesperson, a confident public speaker, or a patient and loving parent.

3. Model the thoughts, feelings, and actions of the version you want to be: Once you have identified the version of yourself you want to become, start modeling their thoughts, feelings, and actions. This means thinking, feeling, and behaving in the same way that person would. For example, if you want to become a top-selling salesperson, start thinking about what they would think, feeling what they would feel, and doing what they would do.

4. Literally be it(Become Worthy of It:):- Make the new identity a part of who you are. Start embodying the traits and qualities of the new identity until they become second nature. This means changing your behavior, your thought patterns, and your habits until they align with the new identity. The second principle of making an identity shift is to focus on becoming worthy of the things that you want in life. Whether you are seeking financial success, meaningful relationships, or a fulfilling career, it is essential to work on yourself first and foremost. This means developing the skills, knowledge, and mindset necessary to achieve your goals.

For example, if you want to become a successful entrepreneur, you need to become knowledgeable about your industry and develop the skills needed to run a business. You also need to cultivate a growth mindset, which means embracing failure as a learning opportunity and being willing to take risks. When you become worthy of success, you will naturally attract the opportunities and resources needed to achieve your goals.

Similarly, if you want to attract positive, healthy relationships into your life, you need to work on becoming the kind of person that others want to be around. This means developing qualities such as empathy, compassion, and self-awareness. By focusing on self-improvement, you will naturally attract people who appreciate and value these traits.

5. Watch as it becomes your dominant reality: Over time, the new identity will become your dominant reality. You will start seeing yourself as the person you have always wanted to be, and your behavior and actions will align with that identity.

6. Embrace the discomfort: It's important to note that shifting your identity can be uncomfortable at first. You may feel like you are leaving your comfort zone and entering uncharted territory. However, this discomfort is a necessary part of the process. By embracing it and pushing through it, you will expand your comfort zone and become the person you want to be.

Example: Let's say you want to become a confident public speaker. You start by becoming aware of your self-image and realizing that you see yourself as a nervous and anxious speaker.

You then identify the version of yourself you want to become - a confident and charismatic speaker.

Next, you start modeling the thoughts, feelings, and actions of a confident public speaker. You start visualizing yourself as a confident speaker, feeling the rush of excitement and adrenaline that comes with speaking in front of a crowd, and practicing your speaking skills regularly.

You then make this new identity a part of who you are. You start speaking up more often, volunteering for opportunities to speak in public, and pushing yourself to take risks and challenge yourself.

Over time, the new identity becomes your dominant reality. You start seeing yourself as a confident speaker, and your behavior and actions align with that identity. You are no longer held back by fear and anxiety, but instead feel empowered to speak in front of any crowd.

CHAPTER 10
RAISE YOUR VIBRATION(FREQUENCY)

Raise Your Vibration: Aligning Your Frequency for Greater Harmony and Joy

Everything in the universe is made up of energy vibrating at different frequencies, including us. When we talk about raising our vibration, we mean tuning ourselves to a higher frequency, one that aligns with greater harmony, joy, and abundance.

So how can we do that? It all starts with alignment.

Alignment means bringing all aspects of yourself into harmony and alignment with your higher self or soul. When you are aligned, you feel a sense of ease and flow in your life, as if everything is falling into place. You are in tune with your intuition and your inner guidance, and you make decisions that feel right for you.

Alignment also means being in alignment with your values, your purpose, and your passions. When you are living in accordance with these things, you feel a deep sense of fulfillment and purpose in your life.

But what does alignment have to do with raising your vibration? It all comes down to the idea that like attracts like. When you are in a high vibration, you naturally attract more high-vibration experiences, people, and opportunities into your life. On the other hand, when you are in a low vibration, you tend to attract more of the same.

Think of it like tuning a radio. If you want to listen to a particular station, you need to tune your radio to the frequency of that station. If you're tuned to a different frequency, you won't be able to hear the station you want. The same is true for your vibration. If you want to experience joy, abundance, and harmony, you need to tune yourself to the frequency of those experiences.

So how can you do that? Here are a few tips for aligning your vibration and raising your frequency:

Practice mindfulness and self-awareness. One of the keys to alignment is being present and aware of your thoughts, feelings, and actions. When you are mindful, you can recognize when you are out of alignment and make the necessary adjustments.

Connect with your inner guidance. Whether you call it your intuition, your higher self, or something else, we all have an inner guidance system that can help us align with our true selves. Take time to listen to that inner voice and follow its guidance.

Align with your values and purpose. When you are living in accordance with your values and purpose, you feel a deep sense of alignment and fulfillment. Take time to reflect on what matters most to you and how you can align your life with those things.

Surround yourself with high-vibration people and experiences. Like attracts like, so seek out people and experiences that uplift and inspire you. This might mean spending time in nature, practicing yoga or meditation, or simply spending time with people who make you feel good.

Practice gratitude and positivity. Gratitude and positivity are powerful tools for raising your vibration. When you focus on what you are grateful for and approach life with a positive mindset, you naturally attract more positive experiences into your life.

Here are some ways to increase your positive vibes and feel better:

• **Being grateful:** You can start a gratitude journal and write down things you are thankful for.

• **Laughing:** You can try laughing yoga or simply dance and have fun!

• **Practicing yoga:** This can help you relax and increase your positivity.

• **Meditating:** Focusing on deep, slow abdominal breathing can help you calm down and feel more centered.

• **Taking a bath:** A relaxing bath can help you de-stress and improve your mood.

• **Walking in nature:** Taking a walk in a natural setting can be very calming and grounding.

• **Going back to happy moments:** Think of a happy moment in your past and relive it in your mind.

• **Listening to music:** Listening to your favorite songs can be a great mood booster.

CHAPTER 11

SHADOW WORK(HEALING YOUR INNER CHILD)

Shadow work is the process of delving into the darker aspects of our psyche, exploring the parts of ourselves that we often try to ignore or suppress. It can be a difficult journey, but it is an essential one for those seeking true healing and personal growth. One aspect of shadow work is healing our inner child. Our inner child is the part of us that holds all of the emotions and experiences from our childhood, both positive and negative. If these experiences were traumatic or painful, it can lead to deep emotional wounds that can impact us well into adulthood. In this article, we will explore the concept of shadow work and the importance of healing our inner child.

What is Shadow Work?

Shadow work is a process of self-discovery that involves exploring our subconscious mind and uncovering the parts of ourselves that we have buried deep inside. These can include repressed emotions, negative beliefs, and past traumas that we may have tried to forget or ignore. The goal of shadow work is not to eliminate these aspects of ourselves, but rather to integrate them into our conscious awareness so that we can better understand ourselves and our behavior.

Why is Shadow Work Important?

There are many benefits to shadow work, including increased self-awareness, greater emotional stability, and improved relationships with others. When we are willing to look at the parts of ourselves that we have been hiding from, we can begin to heal old wounds and transform negative patterns of behavior. Shadow work can also help us to develop greater empathy and understanding for others, as we come to recognize the complexity of human nature.

What is the Inner Child?

Our inner child is the part of us that represents our earliest experiences and emotions. It is the part of us that is playful, curious, and imaginative. It is also the part of us that can be wounded by negative experiences such as neglect, abuse, or abandonment. When our inner child is wounded, it can lead to a range of emotional and psychological issues, including low self-esteem, anxiety, depression, and difficulty forming healthy relationships.

How Does the Inner Child Get Wounded?

The inner child can be wounded in many ways, including physical and emotional abuse, neglect, abandonment, or simply being raised in an environment that did not provide a safe and nurturing space for emotional growth. When our needs are not met as children, we may learn to suppress our emotions and adapt to the needs of others in order to survive. This can lead to a disconnection from our true selves and a sense of feeling lost or disconnected as adults.

Healing the Inner Child through Shadow Work

Healing the inner child is an essential part of shadow work. It involves acknowledging the pain and trauma that we experienced as children, and learning to nurture and care for ourselves in a way that we may not have received as children. There are several steps that we can take to begin the process of healing our inner child.

Acknowledge the Pain

The first step in healing our inner child is acknowledging the pain and trauma that we experienced as children. This can be a difficult process, as it may involve revisiting painful memories or emotions that we have tried to suppress. However, it is important to remember that acknowledging our pain is a necessary step in the healing process.

Connect with Your Inner Child

The next step is to connect with your inner child. This can be done through visualization, meditation, or simply taking time to reflect on your childhood experiences. It may also involve engaging in activities that bring you joy and connect you with your playful and imaginative side.

Nurture Your Inner Child

Once you have connected with your inner child, it is important to nurture and care for them in a way that you may not have received as a child. This can involve simple acts of Self-Love.

How to heal your inner child?

It's vital to be present with our feelings and emotions and pay attention to what they are trying to teach us, rather than attempting to change them. This procedure may be considered as integrating rather than healing. In order to thoroughly experience and examine your feelings, sensations, and emotions in your body, set aside at least 20 minutes each day, as well as at times of very strong emotional reactions. You can notice them getting stronger as you pay attention to them. Breathe through your nostrils without taking any extraneous breaks. Simply and completely be with your feelings and with who you are. If you'd like, you might speak a short mantra to your feelings, such "I am completely here."

It's crucial to remember that this technique works for both happy and negative emotions, not just the former. It might be simpler for some people to cope with negative than good feelings.

Even though it is unpleasant, after thoroughly feeling the emotion, you can explore deeper into its causes by posing the following three questions to yourself:

1. What am I feeling? This enables you to recognise what is going inside of you and bring the feelings into your conscious awareness.

2. When was the last time I felt this exact same way? Allow your being to spontaneously give the solution without consciously looking for it, as if a stream were bringing it to you.

3. When was the first time in my life that I felt this way? Once more, allow the solution to come to you spontaneously, like a torrent washing it downstream, without actively seeking it.

Be patient and trust the process if no immediate solutions present themselves. Have trust that when the time is right, you will learn the appropriate lessons. When you come across emotionally distressing memories, observe them first before mentally modifying them to promote emotional well-being. This method is referred to as "inner child work." For instance, if you remember a time when your father abandoned you, picture your adult self going to your inner child, comforting them, and attending to their needs. You can either develop into a dependable father figure for your inner kid or let them choose one. To help the youngster from taking the action personally, you may also explain the matter to them objectively.This type of memory modification changes the underlying trauma and the way it has impacted your emotional experiences. It enables you to alter your emotional framework.

Writing about your experience of "being with your feeling body" might be beneficial since it shows that you are taking care of your emotional needs as well as making the experience easier to comprehend and integrate. It's crucial to remember that trauma experienced before you learned to speak could be difficult to express in words. But keep in mind that integration doesn't require verbalization or conceptualization.

Strong emotional responses are a sign that earlier traumas have been reactivated. Being with our emotions enables us to cognitively separate from the related tale and move our focus from the external trigger, allowing us to concentrate on our internal sentiments. This enables us to identify old scars that are still present in our lives now. The integration of our emotional body and our whole sense of self is ultimately supported by this. True emotional healing includes doing things like this.

CHAPTER 12

PERFECTION IS A MYTH AND FAILURES ARE LEARNING OPPORTUNITY

THE PURSUIT OF PERFECTION

The idea of perfection is a misleading notion that often sets unrealistic expectations. In reality, perfection is subjective and varies from person to person. What may be considered perfect by one individual may not hold the same meaning for someone else. Despite this understanding, we still find ourselves continuously striving for an idealized version of perfection.

For instance, let's consider a project you have been dedicating significant time and effort to for several months. It may feel like an insurmountable task, and you may question whether it will ever reach a state of completion that aligns with your vision of perfection. However, by sharing your work with others, you open up the opportunity to gather diverse feedback and perspectives.

Receiving feedback allows you to gain fresh insights and identify areas that could be improved or refined. By embracing this feedback, you can enhance your project by incorporating different viewpoints and addressing any potential shortcomings. This iterative process of seeking feedback and making revisions helps to move closer to your desired outcome, while also challenging the notion of perfection as a fixed and unattainable standard.

Allow yourself to embrace imperfection and let go of the constant pursuit of perfection. Trying to be flawless all the time can be exhausting and counterproductive. Instead of pursuing perfection, focus on progress.

Perfectionism can also lead to procrastination, as individuals may feel that they cannot begin a task until they know they can do it perfectly. This can lead to missed opportunities and a lack of progress towards our goals. It is important to remember that no one is perfect, and that mistakes and imperfections are a natural part of the human experience.

Failure is a Learning Opportunity

Failures are often seen as negative experiences, but they can be valuable learning opportunities that can lead to growth and personal development. When we fail, we have the opportunity to reflect on our mistakes and learn from them. This can help us to develop resilience, problem-solving skills, and a greater understanding of ourselves and our abilities.

When you constantly strive to avoid failure, you limit your opportunities for growth, learning, and improvement. Failure is a natural part of life and an essential component of personal development. It provides valuable lessons and insights that contribute to your journey towards achieving your full potential.

By releasing expectations of how things should unfold, you free yourself from unnecessary pressure and rigid thinking. Embracing the unpredictability of life allows you to be more open to new experiences, perspectives, and possibilities. It enables you to adapt, learn from setbacks, and explore alternative paths that may lead to unexpected success and personal fulfillment.

Thomas Edison, the inventor of the light bulb, famously said, "I have not failed. I've just found 10,000 ways that won't work." Edison understood that failures were simply opportunities to learn and improve, and this mindset helped him to achieve great success.

It is important to remember that failure is not a reflection of our worth or ability. Instead, it is simply a step on the journey towards success. When we embrace failures as learning opportunities, we can develop a growth mindset that allows us to view challenges and setbacks as opportunities for growth.

CHAPTER 13

HEALTHY BOUNDARIES

Healthy Boundaries: What They Are and Why They Matter

Healthy boundaries are an essential aspect of personal growth and wellbeing. Boundaries help us to establish a sense of safety, security, and autonomy in our relationships and interactions with others. When we have healthy boundaries, we are better able to communicate our needs and expectations, maintain healthy relationships, and protect ourselves from harm. In this article, we will explore what healthy boundaries are, why they matter, and how to establish and maintain them.

What are Healthy Boundaries?

Boundaries are the limits and guidelines we establish in our relationships and interactions with others. They help us to communicate our needs and expectations, and to establish a sense of safety and autonomy. Healthy boundaries are those that are flexible, respectful, and allow for open communication and mutual understanding.

Some examples of healthy boundaries include:

• Saying "no" when we are not comfortable or willing to do something

• Communicating our needs and expectations clearly and respectfully

• Asking for help when we need it

• Taking responsibility for our own emotions and behaviors

• Respecting others' boundaries and autonomy

Why Do Healthy Boundaries Matter?

Healthy boundaries are essential for personal growth and wellbeing for several reasons:

1. They Promote Safety and Security

When we have healthy boundaries, we are better able to protect ourselves from harm. By setting limits on what we are willing to accept or tolerate, we can establish a sense of safety and security in our relationships and interactions with others.

2. They Support Healthy Relationships

Healthy boundaries help us to communicate our needs and expectations, and to establish mutual understanding and respect in our relationships. When we have clear and respectful boundaries, we are better able to maintain healthy relationships that are based on trust, honesty, and respect.

3. They Foster Autonomy and Empowerment

Healthy boundaries allow us to assert our autonomy and take responsibility for our own emotions and behaviors. By establishing limits on what we are willing to accept or tolerate, we can create a sense of empowerment and control in our lives.

4. They Support Personal Growth and Development

Healthy boundaries are essential for personal growth and development, as they help us to identify our needs, values, and priorities. By setting boundaries that align with our goals and values, we can create a sense of purpose and direction in our lives.

How to Establish and Maintain Healthy Boundaries

Establishing and maintaining healthy boundaries requires practice and self-awareness. Here are some steps that you can take to establish and maintain healthy boundaries:

1. Identify Your Needs and Values

The first step in establishing healthy boundaries is to identify your needs and values. What are your priorities? What do you need in order to feel safe, secure, and respected? By identifying your needs and values, you can establish clear boundaries that align with your goals and priorities.

2. Communicate Your Boundaries Clearly and Respectfully

Once you have identified your boundaries, it is important to communicate them clearly and respectfully. Be honest and direct about what you are comfortable with and what you are not comfortable with. Use "I" statements to express your needs and expectations, and avoid blaming or criticizing others.

3. Practice Self-Awareness

Practicing self-awareness is essential for maintaining healthy boundaries. Take the time to reflect on your feelings and emotions, and pay attention to your body's signals. If you feel uncomfortable or uneasy in a situation, it may be a sign that your boundaries have been crossed.

Be Willing to Say "No"

One of the most important aspects of healthy boundaries is being willing to say "no" when necessary. If you are not comfortable with a situation or request, it is important to assert your boundaries and communicate your needs.

CHAPTER 14
FILL YOUR OWN CUP

Fill Your Own Cup: The Importance of Self-Love

No one can complete you; you are already whole. Happiness originates from within, not from another person. When you love yourself, you establish a healthy relationship with yourself, enabling healthy relationships with others.

No one can complete you,You are the only person who can truly complete yourself. If you desire validation, give it to yourself don't seek external validation.

You cannot expect someone else to make you happy if you are not happy yourself. Giving this power to someone else will only lead to disappointment, unhappiness, and sadness. It is an incorrect approach to rely on others for your own happiness.

Expecting someone else to make you happy is akin to expecting them to read your mind and know your desires. Therefore, entrusting someone else with the control of your happiness is like giving them the steering wheel of your car and hoping they will handle it properly.

I'm not suggesting that you shouldn't trust others, but it's important not to rely on them to bring you happiness at all times, as it is not their responsibility to do so.

It is your responsibility to prioritize your own happiness by engaging in activities that bring you joy and making decisions that align with your well-being. So, how can you fulfill your own needs?

It all begins with self-love. It is impossible to be truly happy if you don't love yourself. Start by giving yourself the love you desire from others. Show appreciation to yourself before seeking it from others. Whenever you see yourself in the mirror, take a moment to appreciate yourself. Validate yourself before seeking validation from others.

Let's take an example of someone who struggles with self-love and acceptance. Emily has always been very critical of herself. She constantly compares herself to others and feels like she's not good enough. She believes that if she finds the right person, she'll finally feel complete and happy. But because she doesn't fully love and accept herself, she often ends up in relationships with partners who are not a good match for her. She may settle for less than she deserves or compromise her values in order to keep her partner happy.

On the other hand, let's look at an example of someone who has learned to love and accept themselves. John has worked hard to develop a positive relationship with himself. He has taken time to reflect on his values and goals and has worked on personal growth. Because he fully accepts and loves himself, he is able to approach relationships with a healthy mindset. He is not looking for someone to complete him or fill a void; instead, he is looking for someone who complements his life and values. As a result, he is able to build strong and meaningful connections with others based on mutual respect and support.

So, how can you work on developing self-love and acceptance? It starts with taking a step back and focusing on yourself. Reflect on your values and goals, and take time to work on personal growth. This might mean trying new things, stepping outside of your comfort zone, and embracing challenges. Remember, growth is a process, and it's okay to make mistakes along the way.

It's also important to accept yourself fully, including your flaws. Nobody is perfect, and it's okay to make mistakes and have weaknesses. When you can accept yourself for who you are, flaws and all, you can approach relationships with a healthy mindset. You can extend compassion and empathy towards yourself and others, and build connections based on mutual respect and support.

CHAPTER 15

KEEP LEARNING

Nurturing a Mindset of Continuous Learning

In our quest for personal growth and fulfillment, it is vital to adopt an attitude of perpetual learning. The realization that we don't know everything opens up a world of curiosity and wonder, keeping our minds hungry for new knowledge and experiences. Rather than settling into a monotonous routine, we should strive to learn something new each day and break free from the trap of sameness.

Learning is a lifelong pursuit that nourishes our minds and expands our horizons. When we engage in any learning activity, our minds absorb information, but it doesn't stop there. Upon revisiting the same material or concepts, our minds grasp new insights or find fresh perspectives, allowing for continuous growth and understanding. The feeling of "I got it this time, now I know" is often followed by the realization that there is still more to learn. Every moment presents an opportunity for new discoveries and personal development.

It's essential to recognize that learning is an ongoing process, not a destination. Success, too, is not a fixed endpoint but a journey filled with milestones and accomplishments. We may set goals, thinking that achieving them will bring us lasting happiness or success. However, once we reach those milestones, our minds naturally seek new knowledge and challenges. The pursuit of success is a dynamic process that demands continuous learning, adaptation, and evolution.

By embracing the mindset of constant learning, we open ourselves to the richness of life's experiences. We find joy in exploring new subjects, acquiring new skills, and expanding our knowledge. Rather than striving for a singular destination, we embrace the ever-evolving journey of learning. Each moment becomes an opportunity to uncover new insights, challenge our beliefs, and discover untapped potential.

Remember, success is not a final stop but a series of milestones along the way. It is the continuous pursuit of learning, coupled with gratitude for the present moment, that allows us to experience true fulfillment. So, embark on this lifelong journey of learning, always seeking new knowledge, embracing change, and finding inspiration in the constant growth of your own mind.

Why is Continuous Learning Important?

There are many reasons why lifelong learning is essential for personal and professional growth:

1. Continuous learning ensures that we stay relevant and competitive in a fast-paced world.

2. Engaging in lifelong learning fuels personal growth, broadening our perspectives and understanding.

3. Continuous learning improves our problem-solving skills, enabling us to tackle challenges more effectively.

4. The process of continuous learning boosts our confidence and self-assurance in various aspects of life.

5. Continuous learning opens up new opportunities and career paths, expanding our horizons and potential.

Making Continuous Learning a Priority:

While lifelong learning is essential for personal and professional growth, it can be challenging to make it a priority in our busy lives. Here are some tips for making lifelong learning a non-negotiable part of your routine:

1. Set specific goals and create a plan to stay motivated.

2. Dedicate regular time each week for learning activities.

3. Take advantage of online learning opportunities.

4. Connect with a learning community to enhance your experience.

5. Embrace new experiences and step out of your comfort zone.

CHAPTER 16
DISCOVER THE TRANSFORMATIVE IMPACT OF FORGIVENESS AND NON-JUDGMENT

Forgiveness and non-judgment are two essential qualities that can bring peace and harmony to our lives. Yet, many of us struggle to let go of grudges and judgments, leading to feelings of anger, resentment, and bitterness. In this article, we'll explore the importance of forgiveness and non-judgment and provide some tips on how to cultivate these qualities in our lives.

The Importance of Forgiving Others

Forgiveness is the act of releasing anger, resentment, or bitterness towards someone who has wronged us. It is not about forgetting or condoning the actions of others, but rather about freeing ourselves from the emotional burden of holding onto negative feelings.

Here are some reasons why forgiving others is important:

1. It Can Improve Our Relationships

When we forgive others, we open up the possibility for healing and reconciliation in our relationships. By letting go of negative feelings, we can move towards a place of understanding, empathy, and connection with others.

2. It Can Improve Our Mental Health

Holding onto negative emotions like anger and resentment can have a detrimental effect on our mental health. It can lead to anxiety, depression, and stress. Forgiveness, on the other hand, can lead to a sense of peace and emotional healing.

3. It Can Help Us to Let Go of the Past

When we hold onto grudges, we keep ourselves stuck in the past. Forgiveness can help us to let go of the past and move forward with a sense of freedom and hope.

4. It Can Increase Our Empathy and Compassion

Forgiveness requires us to put ourselves in someone else's shoes and see things from their perspective. This can increase our empathy and compassion towards others and help us to build more positive and fulfilling relationships.

Why Non-Judgment is Important

Non-judgment is the practice of refraining from making negative judgments or assumptions about others. It involves accepting people as they are, without labeling them or trying to change them.

HERE ARE some reasons why non-judgment is important:

1. It Can Improve Our Relationships

When we refrain from making negative judgments about others, we create a more positive and accepting environment in our relationships. This can lead to greater understanding, empathy, and trust.

2. It Can Improve Our Mental Health

Making negative judgments about others can lead to feelings of anger, frustration, and anxiety. Non-judgment, on the other hand, can lead to greater peace and emotional well-being.

3. It Can Help Us to Build More Positive Relationships

When we approach others without judgment, we create an environment of acceptance and openness. This can lead to more positive and fulfilling relationships with others.

4. It Can Help Us to Grow and Learn

When we approach others without judgment, we are more open to learning from them and growing as individuals. Non-judgment can help us to expand our perspectives and understandings of the world around us.

Tips for Cultivating Forgiveness and Non-Judgment

1. Practice Empathy

Empathy is the ability to put ourselves in someone else's shoes and understand their perspective. By practicing empathy, we can develop greater understanding and compassion towards others, making forgiveness and non-judgment easier.

2. Reframe Your Thinking

Try to reframe your thinking about others from a negative to a positive perspective. Instead of judging someone for their flaws or mistakes, focus on their positive qualities and strengths.

3. Let Go of Grudges

Holding onto grudges only harms ourselves in the long run. Try to let go of negative feelings towards others and focus on forgiveness and understanding.

CHAPTER 17
5 STEP CREATIVE PROCESS OF LOA

The journey towards manifesting your desires and achieving your goals involves a 5-step creative process. By following these steps, you can align your thoughts, emotions, and actions with your desired outcome, effectively harnessing the power of the universe to bring it into reality.

Step 1: ASK - Instead of solely focusing on what you want to acquire, shift your perspective to consider who you want to become. This step involves envisioning the qualities, characteristics, and values that align with your desired outcome. By clarifying your intentions and identifying the person you want to evolve into, you set a powerful foundation for manifestation.

Step 2: Feeling - Embracing the feeling of already having achieved your desired outcome is a crucial aspect of the creative process. Visualize yourself in that desired state, allowing the emotions associated with success and accomplishment to flow through you. Practice visualization techniques both in the morning and at night, engaging in "movie making" where you vividly imagine your desired reality. Utilize tools such as vision boards to visually represent your aspirations. Moreover, start accepting yourself and nurturing self-love, as it is a key component in attracting what you desire. Cultivate gratitude by writing down five things you are grateful for each morning, further amplifying positive energy in your life.

Step 3: Believing - Develop a strong belief in your worthiness to receive the manifestation of your desires. Affirm to yourself that you deserve the abundance and success you seek. Challenge any limiting beliefs or self-doubt that may arise, replacing them with empowering thoughts and affirmations that support your goals. Believe wholeheartedly that the universe is conspiring in your favor.

Step 4: Action and Hard Work - While the universe provides guidance and opportunities, it is important to take inspired action and put in the necessary effort. The universe responds to your dedication and commitment. Trust the signs and synchronicities that the universe presents, and follow the path it guides you on. Take consistent action towards your goals, utilizing your skills and talents to propel yourself forward.

Step 5: Receiving - Open yourself to receiving the manifestation of your desires. Stay in a state of receptivity and remain open to the abundance and opportunities that come your way. Allow yourself to receive and acknowledge the gifts that the universe presents to you. Maintain a positive mindset, gratitude, and appreciation as you witness the manifestation of your desires unfolding.

By implementing this 5-step creative process, you can actively participate in shaping your reality. Remember that the key lies in aligning your thoughts, emotions, beliefs, and actions with your desired outcome. Embrace this process as a journey of self-discovery, personal growth, and transformation. The universe is ready to support you on this path towards manifesting your dreams.

CHAPTER 18

ATTRACT MONEY

UNIVERSE IS ABUNDANT AND LIMITLESS

When it comes to attracting money, it's important to understand that the universe is abundant and limitless. There's no shortage of what the universe can provide, including money. The money you desire is already out there in the vastness of the universe, just waiting for you to claim it. All you need to do is state your intention and have unwavering belief that it's possible. It's like giving the universe your address, signaling that you're open and ready to receive the financial abundance you desire. Trust in the abundance of the universe and believe that the money you seek is already within reach.

IDENTIFY YOUR MONEY BLOCK BELIEFS

It's crucial to take the time to identify and understand any money block beliefs that may be affecting your financial abundance. These beliefs are often deeply ingrained and can stem from various sources such as family upbringing, cultural conditioning, or past experiences. They may include thoughts like "money is hard to come by," "I'm not worthy of financial success," or "rich people are greedy." By delving deeper into these beliefs, you can uncover their roots and begin to challenge and release them. This process involves self-reflection, introspection, and a willingness to confront any fears or insecurities related to money. Once you become aware of these limiting beliefs, you can consciously replace them with positive and empowering thoughts. Embracing a mindset of abundance means recognizing that there is more than enough wealth and prosperity to go around. It involves cultivating gratitude, trust, and a sense of deservingness for financial abundance. By releasing money block beliefs and adopting a mindset of abundance, you create a fertile ground for attracting wealth and allowing prosperity to flow effortlessly into your life.

THE MORE YOU GIVE, THE MORE YOU RECEIVE

By being generous and giving to others, you create a positive energetic flow that attracts abundance back into your life. It's not just about material giving, but also about giving in terms of time, knowledge, support, and kindness. When you give freely and selflessly, without expecting anything in return, you align yourself with the energy of abundance. This mindset shift opens up opportunities, fosters positive relationships, and enhances your reputation, all of which can lead to financial rewards. By being open-hearted and generous, you create a virtuous cycle where the more you give, the more you receive.

When we give, we create a positive energy that attracts more positivity and abundance into our lives. This can be done in many ways, such as donating to charity, volunteering, or simply giving compliments or acts of kindness to others. By giving, we also cultivate a sense of gratitude and abundance that can attract more wealth into our lives.

It's important to note that the act of giving should come from a genuine place of kindness and generosity, rather than a desire to receive something in return. When we give with a pure heart, we create a positive energy that can benefit both ourselves and those around us.

THE UNIVERSE IS A MIRROR

The universe operates as a mirror, reflecting back to you the energy and beliefs you emit. If you radiate scarcity or lack, that is what you will receive. However, by cultivating a mindset of abundance and gratitude, the universe mirrors these vibrations and presents you with opportunities for financial growth and prosperity. So if you have a mindset of lack or scarcity, that's what you'll attract. But if you focus on abundance, gratitude, and positivity, the universe responds by bringing more opportunities for financial success your way. It's about aligning your thoughts, actions, and beliefs with the kind of prosperity you want to experience.

Rich Mindset:

Believes in personal control: Rich people believe that they have the ability to take control of their lives and shape their own destinies. They understand that their actions and decisions directly impact their financial success.

Committed to achieving wealth: They are dedicated to actively pursuing wealth and take consistent action towards their financial goals. They are willing to invest time, effort, and resources to build their wealth.

Thinks big: Rich individuals have a mindset of abundance and think beyond limitations. They set ambitious goals and are not afraid to dream big. They focus on expanding their wealth and exploring new opportunities.

Focuses on opportunities: They have a keen eye for spotting opportunities in various areas, whether it's in business, investments, or personal development. They proactively seek ways to grow their wealth and capitalize on favorable circumstances.

Admires and learns from the rich: Rich people surround themselves with successful individuals and admire their achievements. They understand the value of learning from those who have already achieved financial success and use their examples as inspiration.

Poor Mindset:

Believes control is external: Poor individuals often believe that external circumstances or other people have control over their financial situation. They may feel powerless to change their circumstances and rely on external factors to determine their financial outcomes.

Desires wealth without action: While desiring wealth, poor people may not take consistent action or make necessary efforts to improve their financial situation. They may have a passive approach and expect wealth to come without actively working towards it.

Thinks small or middle-class: The poor mindset often limits one's aspirations to a small or middle-class level. They may have limited beliefs about what is possible and shy away from pursuing bigger opportunities or financial growth.

Focuses on problems: Instead of seeking solutions, the poor mindset tends to dwell on problems and challenges. They may perceive obstacles as insurmountable and focus on the difficulties rather than exploring ways to overcome them.

Jealous of the rich: Poor individuals may feel envy or resentment towards those who are financially successful. Rather than admiring and learning from the rich, they may develop negative emotions and attitudes towards them.

It's important to note that these characteristics are generalizations and not applicable to every individual. Mindsets can change, and anyone can work towards adopting a more empowering mindset that aligns with financial abundance.

CHAPTER 19
MANIFESTING THE IDEAL LIFE PARTNER

Nurture self-love within yourself before anticipating love from others.

In order to attract an amazing life partner, it is important to focus on oneself and strive to become the best version of oneself before entering into a romantic relationship. So before you can find that special someone, it's important to take care of yourself and do some serious soul-searching. This means figuring out what makes you tick, what makes you happy, and what you really want in a partner and in life.

By working on yourself and growing as an individual, you become more confident and comfortable in your own skin. You radiate positive vibes and attract people who appreciate and value you for who you are. It's like having a secret magnet that draws in fantastic potential partners.

Attracting a life partner also means taking care of your well-being. You got to treat yourself with love and kindness, both physically and emotionally. This involves doing things that make you feel good, setting boundaries, and surrounding yourself with positivity.

But here's the best part: attracting a life partner isn't about changing yourself or pretending to be someone you're not. It's about embracing your quirks and uniqueness. When you're true to yourself, you attract someone who loves and accepts you for exactly who you are.

So, focus on being the best version of yourself, have fun, and enjoy the journey. By attracting positivity and investing in your own happiness, you'll attract a remarkable life partner who fits perfectly into your world. You've got this!

Intention for the ideal partner

To attract the right partner, we need a clear vision for the qualities and values we seek in a relationship.

To have clarity about our desired life partner, it's important to set clear goals and intentions. You can envision a happy and fulfilling relationship with your ideal partner by creating a vision board, making a list of desired traits, or simply visualizing yourself in a loving and joyful partnership.

It's important to note that clarity of intention should come from a place of positivity and abundance, rather than a place of desperation or neediness. When we approach attracting a partner from a place of abundance and positivity, we create a positive energy that attracts love and partnership into our lives.

Embodying desired traits

Finally, another important part of finding a life partner is being in tune with the qualities we desire. It means embracing the qualities and values we want in a partner and being open to the possibility of meeting someone who possesses those traits.

For instance, if we want a partner who is kind, caring, and generous, we should strive to embody those qualities ourselves. By radiating these qualities, we attract others who share them.

It's also important to be open to the possibility of connecting with someone who may not perfectly match our expectations but aligns with our values and desires in other ways. By staying open-minded and flexible, we create the opportunity for a fulfilling and compatible relationship to flourish.